ETIENNE-LOUIS BOULLÉE

Etienne-Louis
BOULLÉE
(1728 - 1799)

Theoretician of Revolutionary Architecture

JEAN-MARIE PÉROUSE DE MONTCLOS

GEORGE BRAZILLER

NEW YORK

Translated from the French by James Emmons

Copyright © 1974 by Jean-Marie Pérouse de Montclos
Published simultaneously in Canada by Doubleday Canada, Limited
All rights reserved
For information address the publisher:
George Braziller, Inc., One Park Avenue, New York, N.Y. 10016
Library of Congress Catalog Number: 72–92833
Standard Book Number: 0–8076–0672–3, cloth
0–8076–0671–5, paper
Printed in the U.S.A.
First Printing

Contents

ETIENNE-LOUIS BOULLÉE

The growing interest taken today in the work of the French architect Etienne-Louis Boullée points to a significant change of taste. It means that we are beginning to reconsider our ideas about neoclassicism, which has been too often equated with the most sterile and hidebound academicism.

Boullée's work provides, as a matter of fact, some particularly illuminating insights into that permanent revolution, that great movement of ideas, that violent uprush of imagination which marked the history of the arts in the latter half of the eighteenth century. It helps us to understand how the backward-looking aesthetic of the champions of a return to antiquity was transformed into a forward-looking aesthetic which is not unrelated to that of the twentieth century.

Boullée played a definite part in the anti-rococo movement which, arising in France in the 1760s, answered the desire for a return to classical equilibrium—in other words, to the national tradition so well expressed by the French artists of the seventeenth century.

In the 1770s, when antiquizing classicism was at its height in Europe, Boullée designed some remarkable examples of a return to the grandeur of antique architecture. But he was not the initiator of this style.

He was, however, the principal theorist of one of the

most progressive forms of neoclassical art—the revolutionary architecture which appeared toward 1785. For it was Boullée's later designs which, by their rediscovery of the natural sources of architecture, gave new meaning to the exploration of antiquity.

The Reaction against Rococo and the Return to French Classicism in the 1760s

Born in Paris in 1728, Etienne-Louis Boullée came of a well-to-do middle-class family. His father was an architect, employed as an appraiser in the service of King Louis XV. First young Boullée studied painting under Jean-Baptiste Pierre, then architecture with Jacques-François Blondel (1705–1744) and Jean-Laurent Legeay (1710?–1786). In the course of his career he built little but produced many designs; the abundance and originality of his ideas, expressed in architectural drawings, made him famous and brought him many pupils. Boullée died in Paris in 1799, in the parish of Saint-Roch, where he had been baptized. He seems to have spent his whole life in Paris, apart from occasional stays in his country house at Fleury, a few miles outside the city.

Boullée thus had his roots in a milieu where family and craft traditions were still strong. He is known to have had some reluctance about following the same career as his father. Working in the studio of Jean-Baptiste Pierre, young Boullée took eagerly to painting and felt that there lay his true vocation. It required all his father's authority to make him give it up and consent to train as an architect under Blondel. Jacques-François Blondel was himself the descendant of one of those dynasties of artists which were so numerous and influential in pre-revolutionary France. Originating in Rouen, the Blondels had settled in Paris to improve their fortunes.

For it was only in Paris that men of talent could attract

the king's attention and obtain the commissions by which they made their name. True, the importance of Paris as an art center does not in itself explain Boullée's lifelong reluctance to travel. It is most unusual in this period to find a French architect of any reputation who had not made the traditional journey to Italy, or built a theater or a church in some part of France, or responded to the invitation of a German prince to remodel his residence in the style of Versailles. On the other hand, Boullée had no need to leave Paris, since all Europe found its way there. His master Blondel was surrounded by foreign pupils drawn to Paris by the universality of French art. Conscious as he was of being the heir to a great national tradition, the Parisian artist was not receptive to foreign ideas. More than twenty years elapsed before the neoclassical style created in the international milieu of the Roman school, and known in Paris as early as 1750 through the agency of Legeay, finally triumphed in France.

The school of Jacques-François Blondel speaks for the influence of French architecture in the eighteenth century. Blondel was the outstanding theorist of French classicism. In his *Cours d'architecture*, however, published belatedly from 1771 to 1774, we find only a faint echo of the debate which led, about 1760, to the condemnation of rococo. Blondel was not so strict as certain doctrinarians in banishing the profuse ornamentation of this style; indeed, it seemed to him that some ornament could provide a pleasing variety in interior decoration. Rococo, for him, was a marginal phenomenon, hardly capable of diverting artists from the "grand manner" bequeathed to them by the architects of Louis XIV. Rococo designers like Oppenord (1672–1742) and Meissonnier (1695?–1750) were only decorators—of foreign origin, moreover—who, without much success, had proposed the tortuous designs of their andirons and paneling to the real builders. In his view, the most

12

representative French architect of the mid-eighteenth century was Jacques-Ange Gabriel (1698–1782), true heir to the French tradition by virtue of his family and professional background and by his very title of First Architect to the King, an office he had inherited from his father. The colonnade of the Louvre was considered the paragon of French classicism, and the buildings in the Place de la Concorde designed by Jacques-Ange Gabriel owe a large debt to it.

Trained in the school of Jacques-François Blondel, Boullée there familiarized himself with the classic French tradition as exemplified by Claude Perrault (1613–1688), François Blondel, and Jules Hardouin-Mansart (1646–1708). Their work still provided the principal points of reference in his *Essai sur l'art*, written in the 1780s: "As a young man I shared the public opinion, I admired the colonnade on the east front of the Louvre and regarded this production as the finest thing in architecture. . . . Considering the superb productions of the great men who contributed to honor the century of Louis XIV, stirred by such fine examples and filled with the desire to surpass these artists, if that were possible, by availing myself of their insights, I aspired only to the fame achieved by these rare spirits in that happy period of the fine arts."[1]

"When Boullée began his career, architecture was still overlaid with those bizarre and contorted forms begotten by the bad taste of the day; he struggled against this petty style and did much to put an end to it," wrote the author of the article on Boullée in the *Biographie Universelle*, published in 1811–1828.

Boullée's position on the side of reform was made clear in 1762 in two works which opened the doors of the Academy of Architecture to him and earned him the title of Architect to the King. The first was for the Hôtel des Monnaies (Royal Mint). For several years previously he had been producing designs for the reconstruction of the mint, but in the end the commission went to one of his competitors, Jacques-Denis Antoine (1733–1801). In 1762 he presented a fine perspective drawing of his project at the Academy of Architecture *(Fig. 7)*. Its elevation keeps to the tradition of Hardouin-Mansart: the rusticated ground floor forming the stylobate, main floor and upper story connected by a colossal order, flat roofs concealed by balustrades. Boullée did, however, take into account the criticisms passed on this classical layout by the theorists of the eighteenth century, Blondel and above all the Abbé Laugier (1713–1769),[2] both of them men with a sense of strict design. Laugier advised builders to reserve the order for the bays of the forepart, to group the windows of the other bays in vertical recesses, and to use pediments only in places which actually correspond to a gable. Boullée had this last piece of advice in mind when he crowned the front of the central unit with a blind attic.

His second work was the redecoration of the house of M. Tourolle on the rue Charlot, in the Marais; of this, only the drawing-room paneling remains *(Fig. 9)*. The room must have been approximately square. Each side of the paneling is divided by Ionic pilasters set out in a ternary rhythm: two rectangular doors frame a round-headed mirror. Such architectural paneling on a ternary design was inspired by Mansart's work at Versailles (the queen's staircase, the king's chamber). It remained in fashion until the end of the century; Boullée used this kind of paneling in all his private houses. The drawing room in the Tourolle house was not covered with one of those stucco ceilings characteristic of the first half of the century, but with a simulated vault painted with a mythological subject, as in the Salon d'Hercule and the Galerie des Glaces at Versailles. It is noteworthy that this work, regarded by Boullée's biographers as the manifesto of the reaction against rococo, should have been a piece of interior decoration. Other outstanding works by contemporary artists belong to the same category.

14

Claude-Nicolas Ledoux (1736–1806), for example, in that same year, 1762, gained public recognition with the paneling he designed for the Café Militaire. The implications and orientation of the reform launched by these men confirmed the analysis made by Blondel.

Some witnesses, however, give a different interpretation of that reform. The authors of the biographical notices written after Boullée's death credit him, as a young man, with having contributed "to restore to art the noble beauties of the antique."[3] This belated assertion, made when antiquizing classicism was at its height, is founded on a hasty interpretation of the taste of the 1760s, when ornaments à la grecque were so fashionable. It would be easy to read too much into Grimm's remark, "Everything in Paris is in the Greek style."[4] In the decoration and furniture of the 1760s, Vitruvian scrolls and fretwork had superseded rococo flourishes, and the athénienne had superseded the console table with its curved legs. But these ornamental innovations never amounted to anything like an architectural reform. The love of novelty was not carried so far as to imitate the fine capital of the Erechtheion, reproduced by David Leroy in his Ruines des plus beaux Monuments de la Grèce, published in 1758; its high necking band adorned with palmettes and its powerful volutes did not appear in French architecture until later. Boulée kept to the models of Vignola (1507–1573) and Scamozzi (1552–1616). Festoons adorning oculi, pairs of putti bearing a medallion or a trophy over a door or romping in groups against the background of a mural plaque, strapwork in door- or window-frames, laurel leaves or vine scrolls in friezes, elongated thistles in the spandrels—Boullée's whole repertory of ornament was taken over from the decorators of the previous century.

Historians concur in regarding the closing years of the reign of Louis XV (he died in 1774) as a transitional period in French art. During this period, when what is improperly called the Louis XVI style took form, Boullée was fully occupied with private commissions. From 1763 on, he presented a project for remodeling the Palais Bourbon for the Prince de Condé *(Fig. 21)*; he built the Alexandre House in the rue de la Ville-L'Evêque *(Figs. 10–13)* and the two Hôtels de Monville in the rue d'Anjou-Saint-Honore *(Figs. 14–16)*; he rebuilt the Château de Chaville for the Comte de Tessé *(Figs. 17–20)*; he erected the house of M. de Pernon and that of the Baron de Thun in the Chaussée d'Antin; and, for the financier Nicolas Beaujon, he remodeled the Hôtel Beaujon at Issy-les-Moulineaux *(Fig. 25)* and the Hôtel d'Evreux (the present-day Palais de l'Elysée) in the rue du Faubourg Saint-Honoré *(Figs. 22–24)*. The Hôtel de Brunoy, built in 1774 (the year of Louis XV's death) in the rue du Faubourg Saint-Honoré, marks the culmination and the close of this period *(Figs. 26–31)*. Little is known in fact about the work Boullée did for the Comte d'Artois, which prolonged his activities in the private sector until 1778.

In the preface to his volume of *Plans des plus belles maisons et des hotels construits à Paris et dans les environs entre 1771 et 1802* (1802), Krafft aptly summed up the qualities characterizing French architecture of the recent past: the beauty of the elevations, in the century of Louis XIV; the refined arrangement of rooms, in the first half of the eighteenth century; and, in the latter half, the harmonious combination of grandeur and comfort. The latter is indeed the principal characteristic of the Petit Trianon, built by Gabriel in 1762–64, as it is of Boullée's work, in particular the Château de Chaville, an elegant cubic structure with very much of a contemporary look, the Pavillon de l'Aurore at Sceaux and the pavilions of the Château de Marly, or, even better, his project for the Palais Bourbon in which Boullée reverted to the layout of the Grand Trianon.

These observations are confirmed by a study of the town houses he built in Paris. Except for the Alexandre

House (now much altered), all have disappeared. But they are known to us from prints, contemporary drawings and descriptions of them in guide books; for such in fact was the common courtesy of that day that genteel visitors were readily admitted to newly built residences described in guide books. The interest taken in Boullée's houses is vouched for by many references to them in travel diaries; the English architect William Chambers (1726–1796) went to the trouble of procuring detailed plans of the Alexandre, Monville, and Brunoy houses (Figs. 11, 13–16, 26, 27, 30, 31).[5]

The Hôtel Alexandre was a private house located between a courtyard and a garden, and prolonged by a small wing on the garden side (Fig. 12). The courtyard was entered by a covered passage through the outbuilding on the street. The ground floor of the main building, divided in half by a longitudinal partition-wall, contained the reception rooms; the living quarters on the upper floor were reached by a lateral staircase; the garden wing contained a small apartment of its own. The same general arrangement obtained in the larger Hôtel de Monville (Fig. 16), apart from a few details (stableyard and single-unit house in depth). This layout had been arrived at early in the century by Mansart's followers and approvingly described by Blondel as one of the most characteristic achievements of the French genius. The small apartment at the back, on the garden, is perhaps the only original feature. It is present in all the private houses designed by Boullée; in it he brought together the subtlest refinements of comfort and decoration.

The garden front of the Hôtel Alexandre (Fig. 12) is in the same style as those on the Place des Victoires and most of Mansart's other works. The court façade, however (Fig. 10), is an early example of the application of a colossal order to private árchitecture; it is modeled on the west front of the Petit Trianon. Thus Boullée, following Gabriel, clearly aimed at giving the house a more monumental character. Henceforth, the wings and out-houses on the ground floor are covered with trellis-work or hidden by blind walls, to set off the volume of the main unit. In the latter, the main floor, slightly raised above ground level, is lighted by a French door in each bay. The upper story, connected with the ground floor by the colossal order, is not lighted from the main façade, where historiated plaques take the place of windows. This device enhances the impression of sheer power conveyed by the crowning features, an entablature extending over the whole length and an attic story, which is often blind (Fig. 14).

Moving in this direction, Boullée could not long remain unaware of the limits of French classicism and the resources offered by antique art. The plan of the Hôtel de Brunoy made due allowance for the traditional requirements of comfort and convenience, but it was treated like a temple—crowned with a truncated, stepped pyramid topped by a statue of Flora, an allegorical compliment to the mistress of the house. Though the Hôtel de Brunoy recalls the villas of Palladio (1518–1580) (who was of course the decisive influence in the rise of neoclassicism), Boullée sought to go beyond Palladio and Palladianism and to hark back directly to antiquity, in this case to the tomb of Mausolus at Halicarnassus, many reconstructions of which had been proposed since the Renaissance. It was from the Mausoleum that he got the idea of crowning the Brunoy house with a stepped pyramid.[6]

The work Boullée did in the years 1762–1774 provided him with a valuable fund of experience: here are to be found the themes which he developed later in his theoretical research.

Overhead lighting is the first of these themes. In his eyes, skylights had the great advantage of leaving him free to design the façades without worrying about the distribution of windows. "I have tried to avoid," he wrote, "that thinness of effect which comes of having too many openings. These make the piers too narrow, so that the house is reduced to a kind of lantern of an intolerable monotony."[7] He accordingly eliminated windows from the upper floor of the main façade, and soon came to make all his façades blind. Thanks to skylights, moreover, the architect gains complete freedom in the arrangement of light effects in the interior. The boudoir of the Beaujon apartments in the Hôtel d'Evreux is lighted by oculi placed at the springing line of the false dome; they are concealed by the arching of a second dome which throws the light back over the cupola of the first. The false domes in the Turkish drawing room of the Hôtel de Monville and the dining room of the Beaujon house at Issy-les-Moulineaux are both open at the top; here the interior arching of the dome conceals a gallery for musicians. Whether in response to visual or acoustical requirements, the effect aimed at remains the same: diffusion and illusion. But Boullée was not the inventor of this device. Rather than the domes with an overhead oculus covering Palladio's vestibules or the Pantheon in Rome, Boullée must have had in mind the example set by Mansart who, in the church of the Invalides, in Paris, had been the first to use the double dome.

The second of these themes concerns Boullée's study of the relations between nature and architecture. He might never have acquired the conviction that architecture should imitate nature, had he not first attempted to harmonize a house with its garden. He is known to have been interested in landscape architecture. Very few landscape designs, however, can be safely attributed to him: possibly the English park at Chaville, which seems to be one of the earliest examples of its kind in France; certainly the French gardens of the Beaujon house at Issy and the gardens of the Hôtel d'Evreux and the Hôtel de Brunoy. But Boullée does not seem to have been partial to the English garden; he was too much attached to the

French tradition to welcome imported styles unreservedly. His most famous garden, that of the Hôtel de Brunoy, is original in design. The temple of the goddess Flora must have been surrounded by foliage; from the court an avenue lined with chestnut trees led to the rue Saint-Honoré. The garden was separated from the quincunxes of the Champs-Elysées by a simple fence. To provide a clear view, the garden paths laid out between the house and the public walk were sunk below ground level and covered with a bower of greenery. This sight naturally attracted the attention of passers-by in the Champs-Elysées and it was mentioned in all the guide books.

The vegetation on the trellis-work covering the façades was repeated inside the house, the rooms being adorned with simulated shrubbery in painting or sculpture. The Turkish drawing room in the Hôtel de Monville "simulates a pavilion with a view into Oriental gardens, the tree tops of which are visible between the columns which support the pavilion."[8] The dining room in the Beaujon house "represents a great hall of chestnut trees, with light entering only through the empty space left at the top of the trees forming the vault. . . . at the foot of the trees are painted tufts of hollyhock, and the background is occupied by simulated trellises with baskets of flowers standing in front of them."[9] The rooms facing the garden of the Hôtel de Brunoy and of the Hôtel d'Evreux were lined with mirrors, reflecting views of the garden.

II

The Return to Antiquity
and International
Neoclassicism
in the 1770s

Boullée's appointment in 1778 to the post of General Controller of Buildings at the Hôtel des Invalides opened up the prospect of an official career and gave him hopes of receiving commissions for public buildings. For the architects of that day, such commissions represented the recognition to which they all aspired. From 1778 on, Boullée ceased to work for private clients. It is hardly to be supposed that he suddenly lost favor with them; he must have decided to turn down private commissions in order to devote himself to work which he considered more important. His biographers were fully aware of this transition: "Though his designs [for private houses] reveal an exquisite taste and though they bear the mark of a most fertile imagination, one is tempted to regard them as the fruit of Boullée's spare time when one comes to see a complete set of his designs."[10] In the set assembled to illustrate his *Essai sur l'art*, Boullée included several large projects, designed between 1778 and 1788, which, appearances notwithstanding, are not purely speculative conceptions; in them he dealt with programs which had been officially defined by the public authorities.

Already, with his plan for remodeling the Palace of Versailles *(Figs. 36, 37)*, he entered the field of public architecture. The Versailles of Louis XIV had been much criticized. Most theorists regretted that, in order to envelop the old château built by Louis XIII, which his son wished to preserve, Le Vau (1612–1670) and Mansart had been obliged to adopt a vast block whose sections were too fragmented. Nor was the internal layout satisfactory. The Galerie des Glaces, which should have formed a stately approach to the king, was practically reduced to a private hall between the king's apartments and those of the queen. Gabriel had been commissioned to remodel and enlarge the Palace of Versailles, but progress was so slow that Gabriel's plans had come to seem outmoded even before the work was completed. In 1780 the Director of Buildings asked for new ideas from six architects, including Boullée. In the project presented by the latter, the palace of Louis XIV was entirely masked on the entrance side by a new front of predominantly horizontal design; with the apartments of the king and the queen transferred to two new wings overlooking the garden, the Galerie des Glaces became the center of the layout.

The project for a palace, known from a drawing by Boullée dated 1785 *(Fig. 72)*, does not seem to answer to any specific commission, though Boullée proposed its erection on the site of the château of Saint-Germain-en-Laye, a building placed under the care of the chief architect in the service of the Comte d'Artois, the king's brother—a post to which Boullée was appointed in 1775. This project called not only for a palace for the sovereign, but a series of palaces around it for the courtiers, together with a surrounding wall and two truncated pyramids flanking the entrance—a royal city whose construction the French monarchy, then on the verge of bankruptcy, could scarcely have undertaken.

The project for the church of the Madeleine *(Figs. 38–40)* was "conditioned by the foundations laid by the previous architect," Contant d'Ivry (1698–1777), who had been commissioned to build this large Parisian church. When he died the work had only just begun and he was replaced by Couture (1732–1799). Boullée himself had probably hoped to obtain this post; if so, his project would date from about 1777; and there is nothing in the style of the design which might argue against this dating. Boullée's project might, however, be a little later, for Couture's continuation of the work was severely criticized and for several years his position was precarious.

Having failed to supplant Couture at the Madeleine, Boullée turned his attention to another, even more important building site, that of the new church on the Montagne Sainte-Geneviève (the present-day Panthéon). Possibly he hoped to take over from Soufflot, the architect in charge, who died in 1780. If so, this might account for his project for a Metropolitan Church *(Figs. 41–46)*, dated 1781–1782. It is not influenced by the work completed by Soufflot (1713–1780) and appears to be a purely theoretical demonstration of what could have been done on the site. In the subsequent comments on the project in his *Essai*, Boullée situates his Metropolitan Church on the heights of Montmartre or on Mont Valérien. These doubtless seemed to him the next best sites. Possibly Boullée's project was connected with the competition for the Grand Prix of the Academy of Architecture, whose subject in 1781 was a Metropolitan Church; more will be said presently about this possible connection.

On June 8, 1781, the opera house of the Palais-Royal was burned down. At once an open competition began and attracted the leading architects of the day. Boullée drew up a project that very year, though there is no evidence that he was invited to do so. It was not unusual for an architect to submit designs for a given building on his own initiative, in the hope of attracting attention and winning the commission. Boullée proposed a circular, domed opera house, in the form of a large tholus *(Figs. 47–51)*, to be erected in the Place du Carrousel between the Louvre and the Tuileries. It was something of a tour de force to apply a circular plan to a hall-stage combination, which seemed to call for the traditional elongated plan. But the unusual design adopted by Boullée had the advantage of providing a continuous

23

façade which he could pierce with a series of entrances of equal size, one between each pair of columns. Safety was thus ensured by enabling the audience to leave the hall at any point on its perimeter. But, above all, the irregular alignment of the Tuileries with respect to the Louvre, which had discouraged every attempt to integrate the two palaces in a single design, was skillfully masked by this circular articulation.

The historical background of the project for a Museum *(Figs. 52–56),* dated 1783, is more difficult to elucidate. The subject set in 1779 for the Grand Prix of the Academy of Architecture had been a museum bringing together the products of science and art. But it may be that Boullée was thinking more particularly of the problems raised by the conservation and display of the royal collections. For several years past there had been proposals to convert the royal palace of the Louvre into a museum. Boullée himself had sat on the committees of 1785 and 1786, set up to study plans for remodeling the Grande Galerie. He nevertheless proposed a new, monumental museum, even though he must have known that it had very little chance of being built.

The same is true of his project of 1784 for a Public Library *(Figs. 62–64).* Yet this theme inspired him to draw up a second project in 1785 which shows that he could on occasion combine realism with grandeur of design. This second plan *(Figs. 65–71)* was for a reading room in the Royal Library, which since 1724 had been installed in the former Palais Mazarin (the present-day Bibliothèque Nationale). Boullée's idea was to create a reading room by throwing an immense barrel vault over the existing courtyard. Of all his projects, this is certainly the one which might most easily have been realized.

Other projects on a less imposing scale show the variety of his interests: a hydropathic establishment on the Champs-Elysées *(Fig. 35),*[11] a fountain behind the church of Saint-Eustache *(Fig. 32)*, and a bridge over the Seine opposite the Place Louis XV, now Place de la Concorde *(Fig. 73)*.

In this series of designs, each project conditioned by specific circumstances seems to have given rise to a second, theoretical project which took no account of those circumstances. The project for the remodeling of Versailles was followed by that for the palace of Louis XVI; the project for the reading room, by that for a public library; the project for the completion of the Madeleine, by the project for a Metropolitan Church. This interaction between public architecture and theoretical architecture is a remarkable feature of Boullée's work. For him, as for most of his contemporaries, the highest form of architecture lay in the construction of public buildings, for it was here that the architect found the widest scope for his powers of imagination and conception—in other words, for art. The designing of a public building called for searching thought on the great, abiding principles of art. Boullée put it plainly in his *Essai:* "Once he has become the steward of the public, the artist is lost as far as the progress of art is concerned. . . . It may be thought advisable that, if he is intent on following purely speculative studies, the architect should abandon any concern with money-making. But where is the man who would willingly sacrifice pecuniary rewards? . . . It may be added that this sacrifice should be made easier by the hope of eventually being entrusted with some large monuments."[12] At the age of fifty, Boullée felt that the time had come to take this step. But he was not destined to carry out any of the large projects of which he dreamed. In the realm of practical endeavor he was confined to the most thankless tasks. He built a riding school for the Ecole Militaire; he converted the old Hôtel de la Force, in the rue du Roi-de-Sicile, into a prison; he remodeled the old Hôtel Tubeuf, in the rue Vivienne,

25

when it became the Paris Stock Exchange *(Fig. 34)*, and the old Hôtel de Langlée in the rue des Petits-Champs, when it became the seat of the National Lottery.

Boullée himself cannot be held entirely responsible for his failure to do greater things. Political circumstances were unfavorable to the development of monumental architecture as Boullée conceived it. Under the monarchy, public life was inseparable from the private life of the king, and the royal residence was the seat of the government of the kingdom. In pre-revolutionary France, the great corporate bodies of the State were housed in the wings of the Palace of Versailles; the administration of Finance was dispersed in former private mansions in the rue des Petits-Champs; the king's library and the royal collections of works of art were also housed in what had once been private or royal residences. Since its foundation, the Paris Opéra had been in the Palais-Royal. Until 1767 the Hôtel des Monnaies (Royal Mint) was housed in some wretched buildings in the rue de la Monnaie; there was no thought of providing a proper setting for that symbol of the royal power, the right to coin money. Versailles alone symbolized that power.

The construction of the Hôtel des Monnaies *(Figs. 6–8)* on the Quai Conti in 1767 shows that, in the last years of the Ancien Régime, there were signs of a change in the old ways. But certain forms of art could only develop in the altered climate of the Revolution, which provided the architect with the challenge of new programs and created favorable conditions for public buildings of monumental design. The very idea of a "monument" acquired fresh meaning. In the classic dictionary of D'Aviler, the word still has its etymological sense of a commemorative edifice. In the dictionary of Quatremère de Quincy, it has taken on quite another meaning. Under the heading "Theater," for example, we read: "The Odéon . . . is the

26

only theater in Paris which may deservedly be described as a monument: its approaches, the regularity of the square in which it stands and above all its isolation . . . enhance its appearance." Under "Monument" we find a definition in these terms: monumental architecture presupposes a complete organization of the surroundings and the masses. The classical architects had applied these principles in building the royal residences; it never occurred to them that the design of a theater might merit a similar amplification. A theater in pre-revolutionary France was merely a hall in the annex to a palace; at most, when it formed an independent unit and opened onto the street, the entrance was given a certain elaboration. For Boullée, on the other hand, as his Opera project makes quite clear, a theater was a temple. He spontaneously took over the vocabulary and principles of sacred architecture, the only field in which the monumental style had been cultivated since the fall of ancient Rome.

It was of course to rediscover the secret of monumental architecture that artists turned to the study of antiquity. The style that was to prevail in France in the 1770s had arisen some thirty years before in the international circle centering on the French Academy in Rome: drawing-class exercises inspired by Roman festivities provided the pretext for grandiose compositions which, in the eyes of those who made them, were merely beguiling but short-lived whims.

Among the most notable of these artists was Jean-Laurent Legeay, Boullée's second teacher. While the pupil never left Paris, the teacher wandered all over Europe. Winning the Grand Prix of the Academy of Architecture in 1732, Legeay lived in Rome on a royal grant from 1742 to 1748. After a short stay in Paris, he worked in Mecklenburg and Prussia, where he built the Hedwigskirche in Berlin and the outbuildings of the Neues Palais at Potsdam; he also worked in England. After he returned to France, he published in 1767–1770 his *Collection de divers sujets de Vases, de Tombeaux, Ruines et Fontaines.*

Legeay's pupils number among the most important French artists of the second half of the century. His most influential period as a teacher dates from the stay he made in Paris after returning from Rome in 1748. All contemporary commentators agree in considering his return as an event of cardinal importance for the French school. Legeay imparted to a whole generation the taste for the Roman style, a compound of the strict design of antique art and the baroque grandeur of Bernini. What for the master was only a diversion became for his pupils a ruling passion. When Legeay next returned to Paris about 1770, he was surprised to find that his former pupils "had put up columns everywhere; that was all very well, he said, in the designs for ornaments or fireworks that I set them to copy..."[13] But he himself had shown the way in his own constructions. During his brief stay in Paris, Legeay designed some scenery for the plays which the Jesuit fathers staged each year with their pupils at the College Louis-le-Grand. Boullée was called upon to do the same in 1759, and the scenery designed by the young artist, then still under the influence of his master, combined reminiscences of imperial Rome and baroque Rome (Fig. 1).[14]

Legeay's importance seems to lie above all in the fact that he transformed the practice of design in the architectural studios. Before his time, architects presented their projects in the form of a flat projection, with the result that the client had some difficulty in forming an idea of the effect which the finished work would produce. In urging his pupils to complete the project with a perspective drawing, Legeay probably had no other end in view than that of making it easier for clients and

28

outsiders to understand an architectural design. But in doing so he created the link which had been lacking between the architect and the architectural painter. With Piranesi (1720–1778), the most famous representative of the "Roman school," imagination reigned supreme. Piranesi's fanciful antiquities *(Fig. 2)* strongly influenced the designs of the French school, beginning with those which Legeay himself presented in his *Collection de divers sujets.* The architectural drawing took on the value of a finished work, for now there was increasingly less to distinguish the plan of a fine piece of architecture, the inventions of an ornamentalist, or elaborate perspective drawings from the works of a landscape painter or a painter of ruins.

Most of Boullée's projects can be traced back to a Roman monument. The peripteral rotunda of his opera house recalls the tholi of Tivoli and of the Forum Boarium in Rome *(Fig. 49)*. The project for a Metropolitan Church *(Fig. 42)* imitates the portico of Agrippa's Pantheon; its dome with a skylight is freely transposed in the project for a Museum *(Fig. 54)*. The temples of Baalbek may have inspired the façade of the Public Library *(Fig. 63)*, one of the most characteristic façades of Boullée's later style. Its resolutely horizontal design, with no vertical projections, is emphasized by the entablature and attic which extend over its whole length. The traditional rhythm set by the sequence of bays has disappeared in favor of a single, gigantic, triptych motif: a columned portico between two solid masses, blind and bare.

The transition from his earlier to his later manner can already be traced in the designs for the Hôtel de Brunoy. In the final design *(Fig. 26)*, as in all Boullée's private houses, the emphasis is again laid on the center; the pyramidal mass of the main building dominates the wings. But in a project which he set aside *(Fig. 30)*, we find the horizontal design for the first time: its center is

29

marked only by the semicircular arch which breaks up the entablature of a colonnade covering the whole façade—a design patently based on the elevation of the great court at Baalbek.

The siting and layout of masses in the projects for a palace (Fig. 72) and a monument to the Supreme Being (Fig. 119) recall the great Roman constructions, the Palace of Diocletian at Spalato, Hadrian's Villa at Tivoli, the Baths of Caracalla in Rome, the Temple of Fortune at Praeneste. The distinguishing features are: amphitheatrical siting; tiered, pyramidal design; repetition of a standard module; a hierarchy of functions isolating the center within several enclosing walls. "To impart dignity to their monuments, the Ancients set them in enclosures," wrote Boullée.[15] The centered plan of the Museum, for example (Fig. 52), encloses the entrance porticoes set in a quadrilobed design around the square main building and a Temple of Fame on a Greek-cross plan, its intersection being occupied by an annular colonnade delimiting the central sanctuary.

Since the Renaissance, classical architects had been intent on imitating antiquity. But their knowledge of it was chiefly drawn from the one text available to them, the treatise of Vitruvius, who reduced architectural design to the rule of the orders. The remains then known were themselves judged by that rule. Only a few discerning spirits, in particular Palladio, realized that there was more to ancient architecture than an abstract set of mathematical rules and made their way towards a more exact and thorough knowledge of it. By Boullée's time, after three centuries of archaeological discovery, there could no longer be any question of keeping to the Vitruvian aesthetic. "We read Vitruvius without understanding him . . . ," wrote the architect Peyre (1730–1785). "Though the Romans confined themselves to following the five orders, they varied them endlessly . . . and they were more attached to the principles

30

which they had laid down for the general proportions of *solids* and *voids* [Peyre's italics]. . . . We are beginning to realize that the monuments of the ancients were in a much grander, much more imposing style than anything that has been done since."[16]

The latest discoveries at that time had notably broadened the prevailing notion of Greek architecture, and there was no lack of theorists who maintained that it was time to go back to those who had shown the way to the Romans. But the weight thrown by men like Piranesi on the side of Roman supremacy was still preponderant and compelled the loyalty of French architects. Boullée reproached the Greeks for failing to "stamp their works with a character of their own; their temples . . . all take roughly the same form."[17] Only the Romans had succeeded in adapting architectural form to the underlying symbolic function. "The temple of Jupiter presents a noble and majestic form. . . . The temple of Minerva is characterized by regularity, perfect symmetry and noble simplicity. . . . As soon as one sees the temple of Venus, one longs to enter it; its appealing, rounded form appears to be the handiwork of Cupids."[18] Taking his stand on these dubious archaeological assumptions, Boullée found in them a fresh justification for imitating the antique. In giving his opera house the form of a temple of Venus, his object was to arouse the pleasure instinct.

As against the ideal beauty of the Greeks extolled by Winckelmann, Boullée thus favored the architectural idiom of the Romans. These two trends led in opposite directions and resulted in two conflicting approaches to the antique.

III

The Natural Aesthetic
and the Decline of
Classicism in the 1780s

It looks as if Boullée very soon made up his mind to concentrate his energies on a theoretical definition of his art. The failure of his projects to win acceptance; then, with the Revolution, the closing down of public building sites and the disappearance of aristocratic patronage—all this forced him into retirement and set him writing and thinking about architecture.

The French Revolution has left no great monuments, but it was rich in unfulfilled projects. For some of them Boullée produced designs. His project for a National Assembly Hall *(Figs. 74–77)* probably answered to an idea expressed by the legislative assembly. But the action of the revolutionary government in the field of art was limited to organizing competitions, whose avowed purpose was merely to build up a stock of designs, a "museum of architecture," as Boullée called it.

Circumstances, then, favored Boullée's propensity to prefer architecture "on paper." His chief occupation towards the end of his life was the writing of his treatise on architecture, the *Essai sur l'art*, which was finished by 1793. Some parts of it simply repeat reports or memoranda written after 1780. In the year of his death, 1799, he was still working on his *Considérations sur l'importance et l'utilité de l'architecture*, which was intended to complete the treatise.[19]

In his treatise Boullée set forth, in a coherent body of doctrine, the ideas and aims that had governed his career,

33

represented by a thick portfolio of designs.[20] Some of these designs were made to illustrate the treatise, but most of them seem to have been connected with his teaching activity. For him, teaching was the natural extension of theoretical research. He was nineteen when he began teaching, and he became one of the most popular and influential teachers at the Academy of Architecture. There are some curious coincidences between the subjects set for the Academy competitions and those treated by Boullée; and some striking similarities between the prize-winning designs and Boullée's projects.[21] Yet Boullée's projects invariably postdate those of the prize winners; and since it is unlikely that the teacher copied his pupils' designs, it must be assumed that Boullée has here provided an exemplary summing up and working out of the principles laid down in the classroom before the competition.

It is not too much to say that Boullée achieved a position as one of the guiding spirits of the French school of architecture. The traditional aesthetic had had its day. The rule of the five orders appeared more and more as a sterile, artificial discipline devised by theorists with a limited view of antiquity, who in particular ignored the Doric order with no base, though some new and remarkable examples of it had just been discovered. This massive order showed how far removed the classical ideal of moderation really was from the violent, impassioned, virile ideal of the ancient world as represented by Homer, whose name, in France, meant different things to different critics. Voltaire and La Harpe ranked the classic French authors well above those of antiquity and condemned Homer as uncouth; Diderot, on the other hand, saw him as the source and origin of eloquence. Egyptian architecture was the object of a similar controversy. Quatremère de Quincy, the upholder of ideal beauty, studied it only with a view to impressing students with its uncouth rusticity; Boullée, on the

34

contrary, saw in it an art of elementary volumes capable of producing "the image of immutability."[22]

The way lay open for a revolutionary interpretation of the antique example. Like André Chénier, who cloaked the boldly modernist verse of his poem *L'Invention* under an appeal to the ancients, Boullée hoped to arrive at a universal aesthetic by returning "to the source from which the Fine Arts originated."[23] In this return to the sources, he went first of all to the earlier civilizations antedating Greece and Rome. He had an unusually wide knowledge of these cultures, ranging from the temples of pre-Columbian America to the ziggurats of the Near East, and they opened his eyes to a primitive antiquity common to all the peoples of the earth and unchanging in both its forms and symbols; its archetype was the tower of Babel. The more or less fanciful reconstructions then current of that Old Testament tower inspired Boullée's projects for a tiered tower, a conical tower with spiralling ramps, a pyramidal tower with double ramps, etc. *(Figs. 97–101)*. His projected cenotaphs with their enclosing walls *(Figs. 102–110)* are grandiose evocations of Nineveh and Babylon.

The Newton cenotaph *(Figs. 57–59)*, designed in 1784, is a hollow sphere, its vault pierced with holes through which natural light filters, creating the illusion of stars in the night sky. This design, for all its apparent originality, actually derives from contemporary archaeology. For in the first two of his *Lettres sur l'architecture*, published in 1779 and 1780, Viel de Saint-Maux, a visionary archaeologist,[24] gave a cosmic interpretation of the early temple as reconstructed from ancient texts. He claimed that, originally, the entablature was only a representation of the belt of the zodiac. Astral figures were inscribed on the temple of Bel at Palmyra, and the ancient cosmography was illustrated by the Roman Pantheon and the dome of the Domus Aurea as described by Suetonius.

Funerary archetypes tend to be exceptionally long-lasting. The Mausoleum of Halicarnassus, which inspired the project for a tomb of Hercules *(Fig. 117)*, the mausoleum of Hadrian and the mausoleum of Augustus *(Fig. 120)* are survivals of ancient burial mounds; from them Boullée took over the rows of cypresses which form natural peristyles on his spiral cenotaph *(Fig. 107)* and his Newton Memorial *(Fig. 57)*.

It was from ancient ruins, which provided models for so many picturesque and short-lived buildings in the second half of the eighteenth century, that Boullée got the idea for what he called "sunken architecture." A sunken construction, to his thinking, was one that "is satisfying as a whole, while suggesting to the spectator that part of it is hidden underground."[25] This impression can only arise from knowledge of the complete forms as they exist in traditional architecture. The Funerary Monument "characteristic of sunken architecture" *(Fig. 114)* is a pediment devoid of its portico. Already in his previous designs there was a more or less pronounced tendency to reduce the height of columns in relation to the rise of the vaulting. In the project for the Madeleine *(Fig. 38)*, this ratio is 5:4; in the Metropolitan Church *(Fig. 43)*, it is 1:1; in the Museum *(Fig. 54)*, 2:3; in the Cenotaph for Turenne *(Fig. 105)*, the hemispheric dome rests directly on the ground. The same tendency is evident in the treatment of bays. In the project for the Entrance of a Stadium *(Fig. 87)*,[26] the height of the piers is less than half the rise of the arch over the doorway; and in the project for a Spiral Cenotaph *(Fig. 109)*, the piers have been done away with altogether. This practice was adopted by all the revolutionary architects; early examples of it are to be found in the works of Piranesi, but Boullée alone, the theorist of the school, provides a coherent justification of it.

Early forms are themselves only imitations of natural forms. It was inevitable that, in going back to the sources, Boullée should rediscover nature. "I mean by art," he wrote, "everything whose object it is to imitate nature."[27]

Architecture, as he saw it, is not simply "the art of building"; in describing it in these terms, Vitruvius talked "as a workman, not an artist." The art of building is only the "scientific" side of architecture. "We must conceive before executing. Our forefathers built their huts only after conceiving an image of them: it is this production of the mind that constitutes architecture."[28] In thus separating the mental effort from the execution, Boullée could claim to be reducing the aesthetic of all the Fine Arts to the single principle of the imitation of nature.

This theory resolved all the contradictions which had troubled Boullée since the beginning of his career. Ever since his early days in the studio of the painter Jean-Baptiste Pierre, he had never ceased to regret that he had not become a painter: "Many well-known artists have heard him express this regret, even in his old age."[29] Legeay's teaching, with its continual reference to pictures, never allowed him to forget the vocation he had sacrificed to architecture. Blondel himself advised his pupils "to acquire architectural taste from Raphael's paintings."[30] Boullée followed this advice literally in his project for enlarging the Royal Library *(Fig. 67)*. The "sublime conception of Raphael's *School of Athens*"[31] gave him the idea of assembling all human knowledge under an immense vault, symbol of the universe; like a historic painter, he peopled his design with figures in Roman togas and set out his architectural theme like a scene on a stage. Boullée headed his *Essai sur l'art* with a famous quotation from Correggio: "Ed io anche son pittore" (I too am a painter).

More important were the contradictions which, as a result of his study of primitive architecture, he came to see in traditional aesthetics. Too much of a rationalist to share the views of the relativist aestheticians, he found in the imitation of nature the abiding principle of universal beauty.

Boullée set forth the laws of the beautiful as derived from nature in his "theory of bodies," a study of the properties of objects laying emphasis on "their power to stir our senses, their analogy with our own physical structure. . . . Circular bodies please our senses because of their smooth contours; angular bodies are displeasing because of the harshness of their forms; bodies that crawl over the ground sadden us, those that rise into the sky delight us and those that stretch across the horizon are noble and majestic." He distinguishes two categories of objects: irregular bodies whose "image is mute and sterile," and regular bodies, characterized by symmetry and variety, which are grasped at once by our senses. The most beautiful of natural bodies is the sphere, which combines the most perfect symmetry with the widest variety, for its surface is enhanced by the subtlest gradations of light. Symmetry and variety are the golden rules of architecture. For the notion of proportion, nature substitutes that of scale. "Man in the midst of the seas or carried into mid-air by a balloon has before him a picture of immensity, of inconceivable space"; but if he draws nearer to the sights of nature he sees all things in terms of their relative sizes, "for nature, by assigning its own dimension to each object, has given man the capacity to extend his judgment to everything he views."[32] Thus Boullée gives his designs their colossal aspect by choosing a unit of measure small enough for its repetition "to enlarge the images."

The Newton Memorial is the finest example of what might be called Boullée's "architectural realism." The tiny sarcophagus below is lost in the immense internal space of the sphere (Fig. 58): "It was in the heavens that I wished to place Newton."[33] One design shows the effect by night, when the sarcophagus is illuminated only by the starlight filtering through the holes in the vaulting. Another (Fig. 59) shows the effect by day: an armillary sphere hanging in the center gives off a mysterious glow.

The impression of immensity and immateriality in the internal space is all the more arresting because the spectator is "obliged, as if by main force, to stand at the place assigned to him" (i.e. the lower pole); there, the sarcophagus being the only material point of reference he has, he may well believe himself in a great open plain or on the high sea. This design conveys a highly realistic picture of the Newton Memorial. "It could not be achieved by the customary means of art," declared Boullée; but he does not specify what those means were. The pair of interior views of the cenotaph by day and by night has its counterpart in the two interior views of the Metropolitan Church, "At Corpus Christi" and "During Tenebrae" *(Figs. 44, 45)*. For this latter project, Boullée explains that he has rendered the character peculiar to the different religious ceremonies by "mastering" the light coming from the double dome. In the Newton cenotaph, his creative momentum carried him beyond the technical limitations of his time. He was right in thinking that "the art of building is only the scientific side of architecture," since it was left to science, with the aid of electricity, to provide the means of carrying out these designs.

For Boullée, the great superiority of architecture over the other arts lies in the fact that it is capable of implementing nature. "The power which architecture has of implementing nature comes of its ability in certain cases to do what poetry can only describe."[34] The choice of a site "such as may combine the scattered beauties of nature" is already an artistic achievement. In a section of his *Essai* entitled "Monument of Public Gratitude,"[35] he even states that "the buildings would only be accessories." The poet in him at times prevails over the architect. "The sight of these lovely gardens would fill the soul with pure delight; the charm of these beautiful lakes, mirroring nature, would lend endless variety to the enchanting views; from the doom-laden scenery of these

39

dense groves, these dark woods where the awful gurgle of a torrent rushing from the bowels of the earth seems to bring its groans to our ear, the soul would be filled with conflicting sensations and these would lend further charms to agreeable objects.''

Nature yields its secrets only to the most watchful observer. Boullée carefully recorded all the impressions produced on him by the observation of nature. In the Abbé Batteux's treatise on *Les Beaux-Arts réduits à un même principe* (1746), which was one of the sources of Boullée's aesthetic, we read: ''Before laying down laws, the artist must be a practised observer''; let him imitate the natural philosophers, ''who amass a fund of experiments and then work out a system which reduces them to a principle.'' And in fact Boullée's ''natural'' aesthetic took its methods and aims from the natural sciences. In the Age of Enlightenment, the exact sciences were giving place to the experimental sciences, and an aesthetic of number and ratio to an aesthetic based on sensations. Boullée's library included the works of Bacon, those of Buffon, Valmont de Bomare's *Dictionnaire raisonné universel d'histoire naturelle*, the monumental *Histoire de l'astronomie* by Bailly, and his *Lettres sur l'origine des sciences*. In his study Boullée worked under the portraits of Copernicus and Newton, and the latter inspired the boldest of his designs. ''Sublime spirit! Vast and profound genius! Divine being! O Newton! While you, by the scope of your insights and the sublimity of your genius, have determined the figure of the earth, I have conceived the idea of enveloping you in your own discovery.''[36]

However, since he is unable to reproduce the effects of nature directly, the architect has to resort to symbolic expression. Boullée's designs in the field of military architecture *(Figs. 90–96)* owe nothing to the techniques of fortification: they are simply ''the image of might.''[37] The low mass of his Municipal Palace *(Figs. 78–80)* is supported at the corners by four pavilions serving as guardhouses, because "the foundations of society rest on public strength."[38] Boullée was fond of likening his designs to speeches or poems. Following Condillac, who showed that the arts have their common origin in expression, and Viel de Saint-Maux, who sought in the Oriental languages for the secret of primitive architecture, Boullée regarded his art as a language.

The term "speaking architecture" *(architecture parlante)* has been aptly applied to Boullée's work and, if an amusing ambiguity may be permitted, his work might also be described as "edifying architecture." For in Boullée's view, imbued as he was with the ideas of the sensualist philosophers, architecture is one of the elements in the human environment which shapes the individual, and so it too may contribute to the building and improving of society. In undertaking his designs for a stadium, *(Figs. 88, 89)* he was actuated by "moral and political views"; as he aphoristically put it, "national pleasures help to maintain good morals."[39]

André Chénier's militant poetry had its counterpart in Boullée's committed architecture. His metaphorical design for a National Assembly Hall is notable for its facade inscribed with the sacred text of the laws, which Boullée described as "the object of all men's love, because all men have willed them."[40] This work testifies to his enthusiastic espousal of the "enlightened" revolution of 1789. After all, the revolutionary constitution drew on the same sources as the new aesthetic: antiquity and nature.[41]

The plates and commentary of the project for a Metropolitan Church describe a Masonic ceremony of initiation. The play of light, the initiatory circle, the starry vault and the Great Architect of the Universe are the principal terms of the rite. The Tower of Babel, symbol of division among nations, was taken by Boullée as a symbol of their union. On the design for a Spiral Tower *(Fig. 99)*, a procession of figures with joined hands winds upwards in a spiral bas-relief, perhaps symbolizing the brotherhood of the lodge: "If all men were wise enough to join together in a single family, one would be tempted to believe that architecture was given to them by the Godhead in order to establish mankind on earth."[42] Boullée believed in that "universal religion" whose origins were explained by the contemporary scientific writer Charles Dupuis with his theory that the history "of the Gods is only the history of Nature itself," and that all mythologies are an allegorical account of the great spectacles of the sky by day and by night, of the contest between light and darkness.[43]

Boullée was fond of the word "sublime" and to him, in keeping with the usage of that day, it meant the highest form of the beautiful. But already, under the influence of Burke and Kant, Boullée colored the term with a nuance of the terrific and the awe-inspiring; he refers to "the horrific beauty of a volcano."[44] Like Ledoux, he calls inspiration "that fine delirium, that happy enthusiasm." To be inspired is "to be moved with such overpowering feeling for the object which engages our mind that all the faculties of our soul are set in motion, so much so that it seems about to burst its envelope."[45] Aiming at the rational beauty of classicism, drawn by the forceful character and elemental power of romanticism, and hesitating between irreconcilable conceptions of genius, one cool and calculating, the other instinctive and inspired, Boullée stands on the borderline between two schools.

Conclusion

"Architecture is only at its inception!"[46] This remark by Boullée—and a similar view is expressed by Ledoux—in fact announced a new chapter in the history of architecture. The art of Boullée and his school transcends neoclassicism but shares with it a common concern to explore the past and learn from it. Only the adjective "revolutionary" seems to fit Boullée's school, for it challenged an order which had been accepted by all Europe for three centuries. The parallel between this art revolution and the political revolution was recognized as early as 1800 by the theorists of the academic reaction.[47] The triumph of this reaction explains the oblivion that was soon to shroud the creators of what, in the jargon of the nineteenth-century studios, was contemptuously referred to as "Messidor architecture."[48]

Yet the architecture of the revolutionary period exerted a considerable influence. That it did so was due first of all to the fact that it opened up new lines of development in several directions. Latent in Boullée's paradoxical genius were two contradictory tendencies, well illustrated by the work of two other revolutionary architects, Jean-Jacques Lequeu (1757–about 1825) and Jean-Nicolas-Louis Durand (1760–1834), the latter a pupil of Boullée.

The universality of neoclassical culture, which produced Boullée's synthetic vision of his art, also led to the syncretism of Lequeu. The latter, in his asymmetrical and heterogeneous designs, combined the antique orders, the belvederes of Italian villas, and Gothic tracery and arches steeped in Oriental reminiscences. He coupled archaeology and nature to engender hybrid monsters combining architectural forms with animal heads. The trite symbolism and aggressive ugliness of Lequeu's work must be seen for what they are: a parody of the revolutionary aesthetic. Lequeu reacted against that aesthetic—a reaction which, in its psychological workings, recalls the sense of release expressed in the fashions and morals of the survivors of the Terror, after 9 Thermidor. Lequeu's reaction, however, seems to have led nowhere, unless we choose to regard him as an ancestor of the Surrealists.

Durand's work, on the other hand, exerted an influence throughout the nineteenth century. Draining Boullée's geometry of its semantic content, Durand retained it only as a method of design, one which was to be adopted by the functionalists. Based on the repetition of standard units, either juxtaposed or superimposed, this method pointed the way to the standardization of modern architecture.

The tendency represented by Boullée himself had a more checkered history. His influence made its chief impact during the French Revolution, and particularly in those countries where the new republican ideology evoked an immediate response, Germany and, even more, Italy. But it is not until the twentieth century, with the rise of the totalitarian regimes, that we find a renewed concern with the symbolic implications of architectural design. The Lenin Mausoleum by Shchusev (1873–1949), Tatlin's (1885–1952) projected monument for the Third International, and Albert Speer's (1905–) building projects for Berlin, show some striking similarities with Boullée's designs, though it is by no means certain that the latter were known to these German and Russian artists; indeed, the political context of Soviet Russia and Nazi Germany probably suffices to explain the reappearance of means of expression which are peculiar to committed arts.[49] There are also some close parallels between Boullée and Le Corbusier (1887–1965) in their distribution of light within the architectural space, and between Boullée and Frank Lloyd Wright (1869–1959) in their concern with merging nature and architecture. Yet, after a century of oblivion, can the last artists of the Ancien Régime really be said to have had much influence on the rise of modern architecture? There has been a tendency to overstate the affinities between modern architecture and the progressive views of architectural design set forth by Boullée and Ledoux in their writings. The truth is that, if the expectations of these theorists had been fulfilled, present-day architecture would be substantially different from what it is.

1. Stage scenery for the Collège
   Louis-le-Grand, designed by
   Boullée and executed by De
   Machy, 1759, engraved by
   Poulleau.

2. Piranesi. "Tempio antico."

3. Entrance to the Hôpital de la Charité, rue Jacob, Paris. Design by Boullée, about 1762, engraved by Taraval.

4. Anonymous painting representing the Chapel of Calvary in the church of Saint-Roch, Paris, built by Falconet, De Machy and Boullée (1754).

5. Church of Saint-Roch, Chapel of St Geneviève, 1763.

6. Project for the Hôtel des Monnaies (Royal Mint), Quai Conti, Paris: Plan.

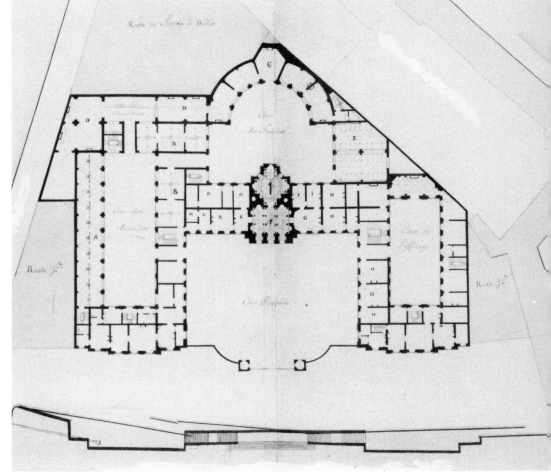

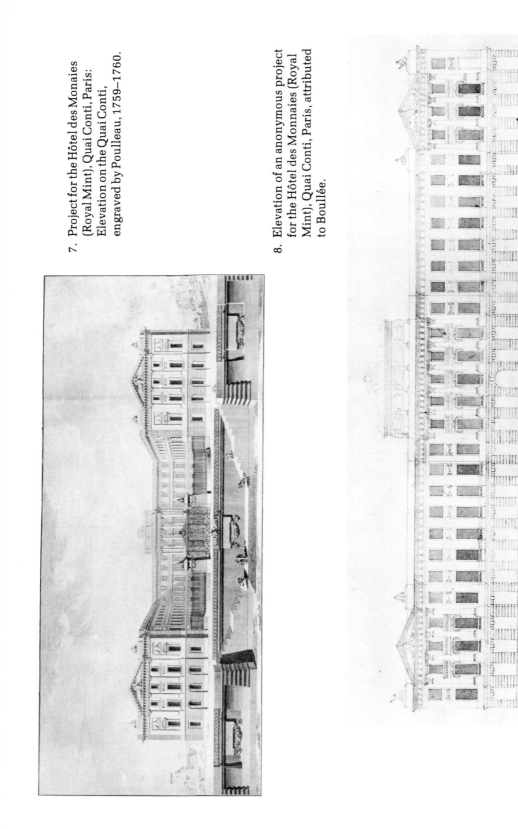

7. Project for the Hôtel des Monnaies (Royal Mint), Quai Conti, Paris: Elevation on the Quai Conti, engraved by Poulleau, 1759–1760.

8. Elevation of an anonymous project for the Hôtel des Monnaies (Royal Mint), Quai Conti, Paris, attributed to Boullée.

9. Tourolle House, 1762. Paneling from the drawing room, now in No. 33, rue du Faubourg-Saint-Honoré, Paris.

10–13. Hôtel Alexandre, No. 16, rue de la Ville-l'Evêque, Paris 1763. Court façade.

11. Court elevation. Anonymous drawing.

12. Garden elevation.
Engraving by Sergent and Roger.

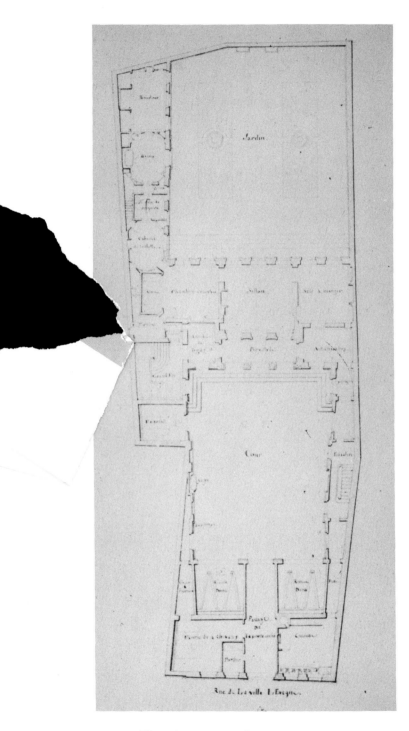

13. Plan. Anonymous drawing.

14–16. Hotel de Monville, rue d'Anjou-
Saint-Honoré, Paris, 1764. Court elevation.
Anonymous drawing.

15. Garden elevation. Anonymous drawing.

16. Plan. Anonymous drawing.

17–20. Château de Chaville
(Hauts-de-Seine), 1764. Final
project.

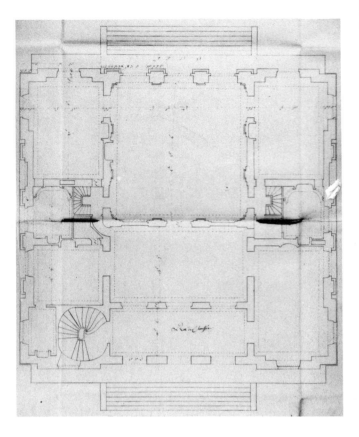

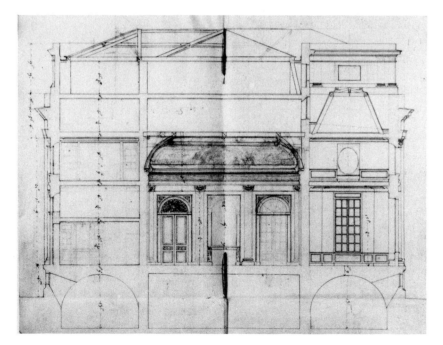

18.

19.

20.

21. Project for the reconstruction of the
Palais-Bourbon, Paris, 1764.
Design made jointly by Boullée and
Moreau le Jeune.

22–24. Decoration of the Hôtel
d'Evreux (now Palais de l'Elysée),
Paris, 1774–1778. Overdoor in the
Grand Salon.

23. Door in the
"Petite Chambre Verte."

24. Panel-frieze in a room on the first floor.

25. Hôtel Beaujon at Issy-les-Moulineaux (Hauts-de-Seine). Paneling from the Grand Salon (present whereabouts unknown).

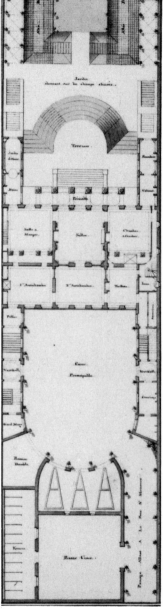

26–28. Hôtel de Brunoy, Paris, 1774.
Garden elevation. Anonymous drawing.

27. Plan. Anonymous drawing.

28. Cross-Section.

29. Project for the Hôtel de Brunoy.
Garden elevation.

30,31. Another project for the Hôtel de
Brunoy. Garden elevation.
Anonymous drawing.

31. *Left:* Plan. Anonymous drawing.

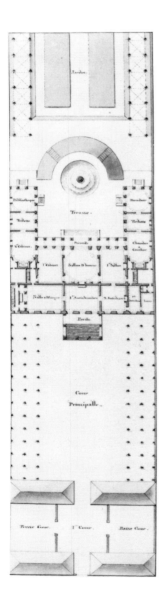

32. Project for a Fountain behind the
church of Saint-Eustache, Paris, in
the square called Pointe
Saint-Eustache. Design dated 1766.

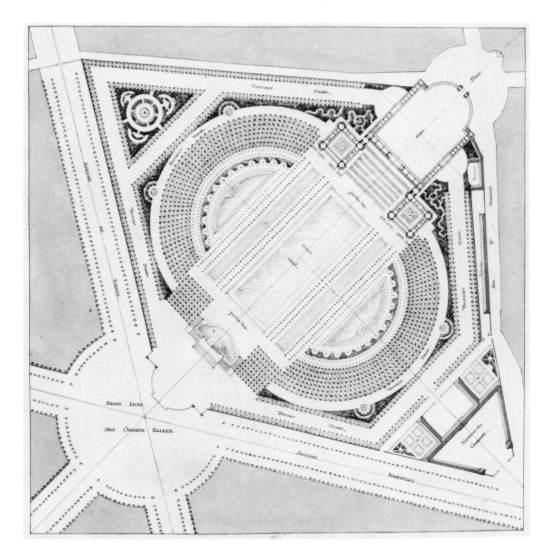

33. Project for a Palace for the Comte
    d'Artois at the Pépinière du Roule,
    attributed to Boullée, about 1780.

34. Entrance to the Bourse (Stock Exchange), rue Vivienne, Paris, 1785, engraved by Durand and Janinet.

35. Project for a Hydropathic Establishment in the Champs-Elysées, Paris, attributed to Boullée.

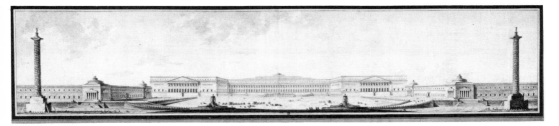

36, 37. Project for the Palace of Versailles, 1780 (?).

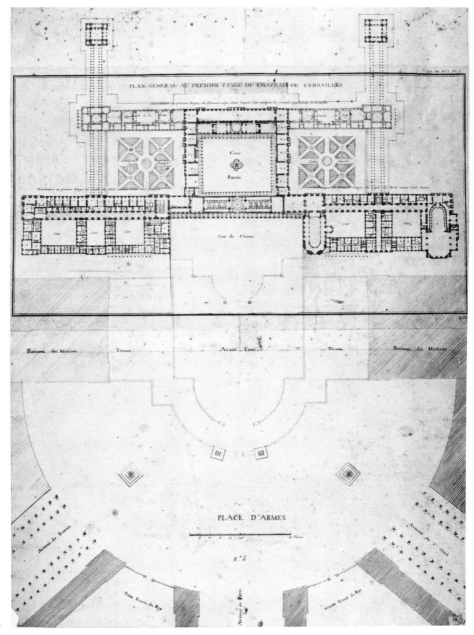

37.

38–40. Project for the Church of
the Madeleine, Paris, about
1777–1781.

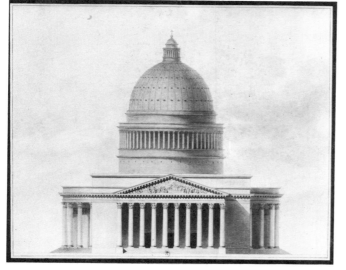

39.

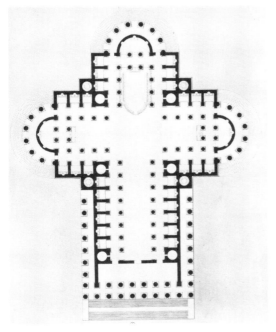

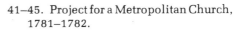

41–45. Project for a Metropolitan Church, 1781–1782.

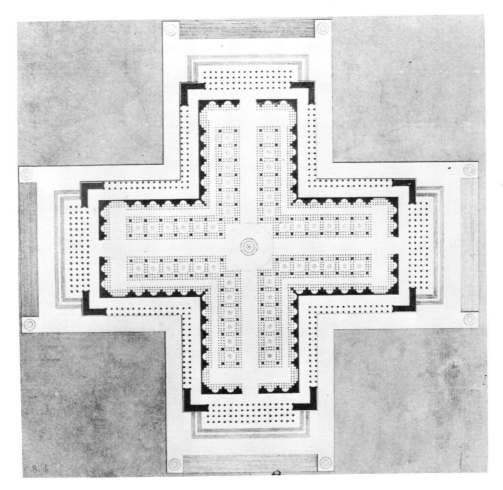

42.

43.

44. "View of the interior at Corpus Christi."

45. "View of the interior at Tenebrae."

46. Variant of the project for a Metropolitan Church.

47–51. Project for an Opera House in the Place
du Carrousel between the Louvre and the Tuileries.

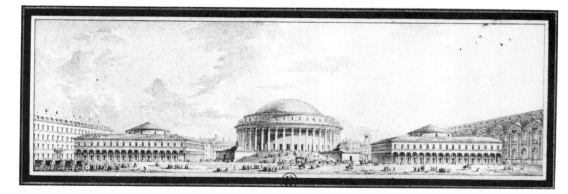

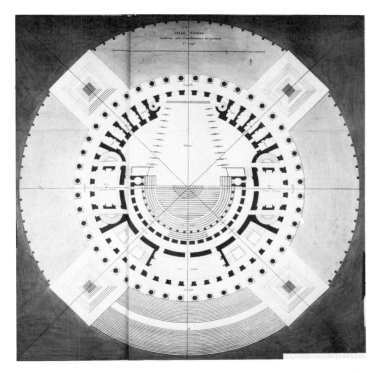

48.

49.

50.

51.

52. Project for a Museum, 1783.
    1. Courtyard, 2. Staircase, 3. Temple of Fame.

53–56. Same project for a Museum.

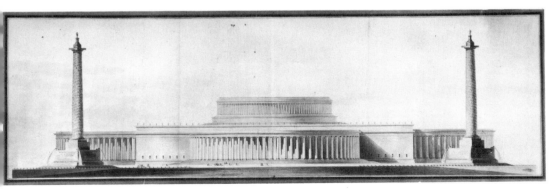

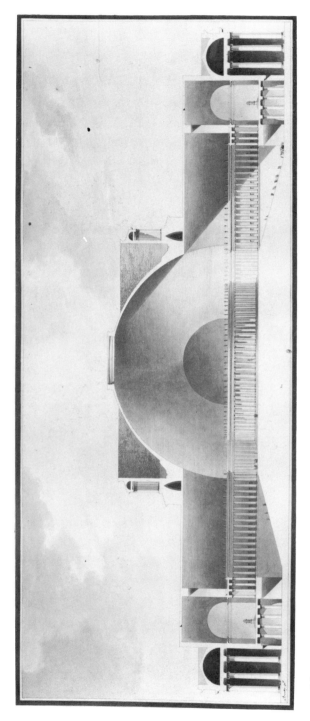

54.

55.

56.

57–59. Project for a Newton Memorial, 1784.

58.

59.

60, 61. Project for a Temple of Nature.

61.

62–64. Project for a Public Library on the site
of the Couvent des Capucines, Paris, 1784–1785.

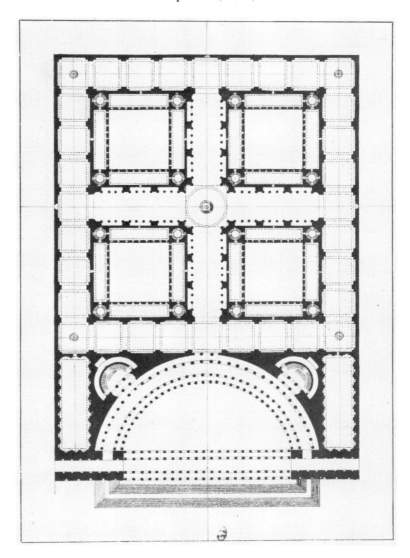

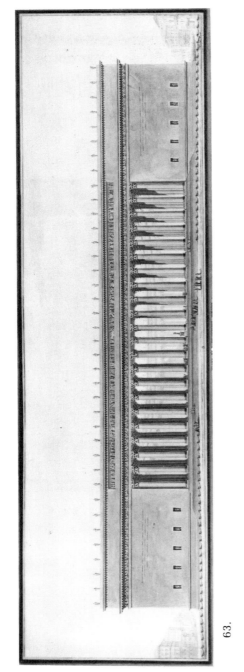

63.

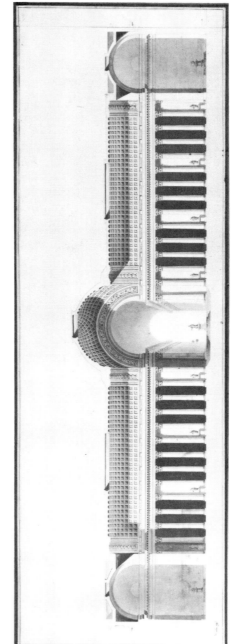

64.

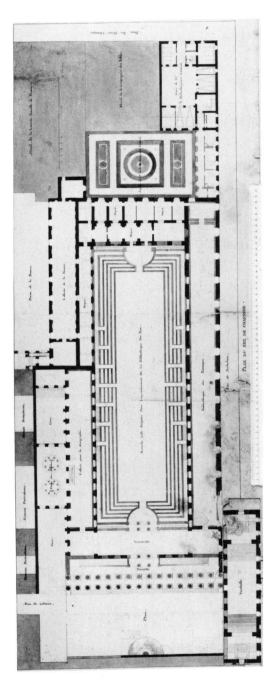

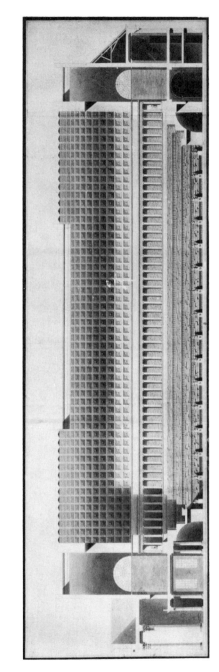

65–69. Project for remodeling the Royal Library, rue de Richelieu, Paris, 1785.

66.

68.

69.

70, 71. Variants of the project for
remodeling the Royal Library.

71.

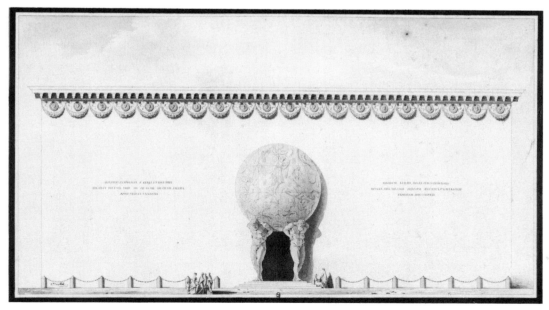

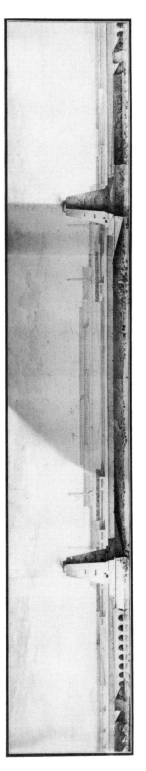

72. Project for a Palace of the Sovereign, 1785.

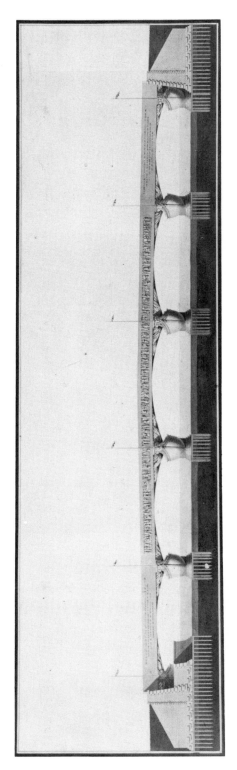

73. Project for a Bridge over the Seine (Pont Louis XVI)
opposite the Place de la Concorde, Paris, 1787.

74–77. Project for a National
Assembly Hall, 1792 (?).

75.

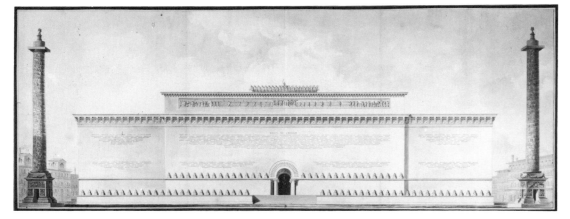

76.

77.

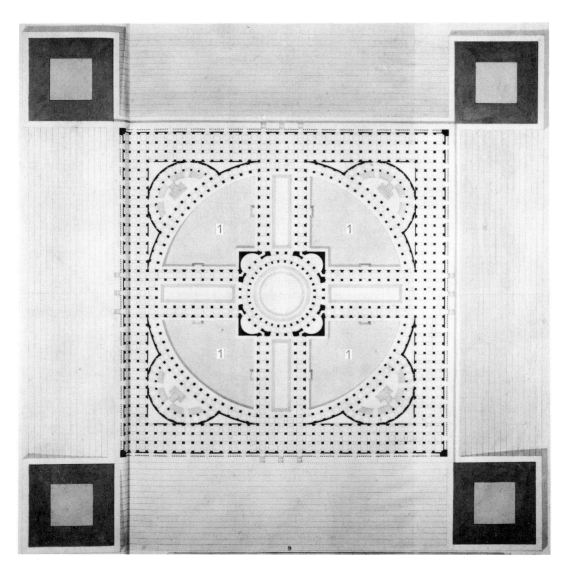

78. Project for a Municipal Palace, 1792. 1. Courtyard.

79, 80. Same project for a Municipal Palace.

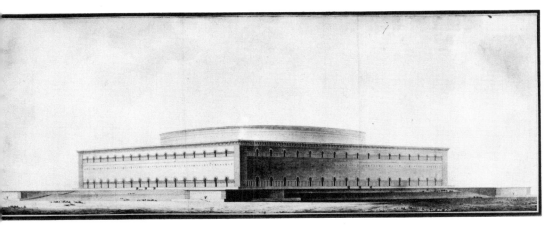

80.

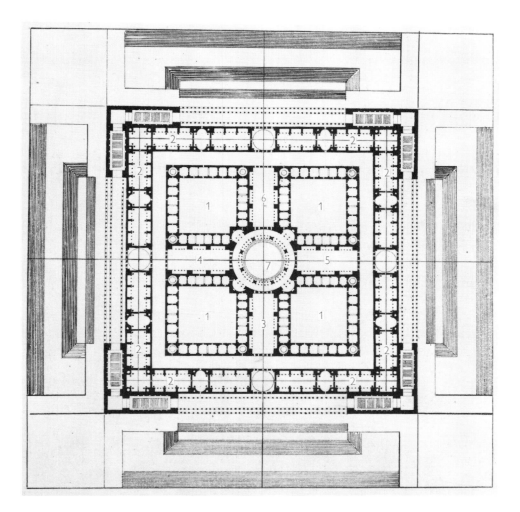

81. Project for a Palace of Justice.
    1. Courtyard, 2. Hall for the different jurisdictions,
    3. Lawyers' Hall, 4. Audit Office,
    5. Board of Excise, 6. Chapel, 7. Law Court.

82. Same project for a Palace of Justice.

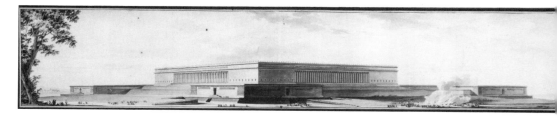

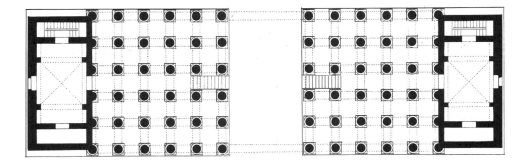

83, 84. Project for an Arch of Triumph.

84.

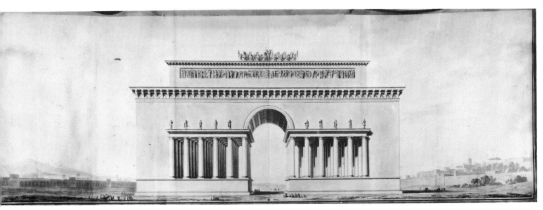

85, 86. Projects for a Triumphal Gate.

86.

87. Project for the Entrance to a Stadium.

88. Project for a Stadium.

89. Variant of the project for a Stadium.

90–95. Projects for a City Gate.

91.

92.

93.

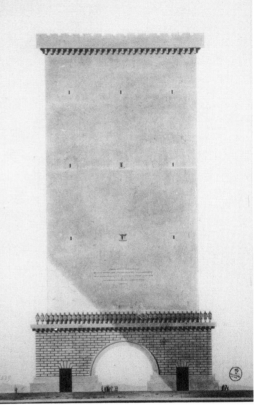

94.

95.

96. Project for a Fort.

97, 98. Projects for a Lighthouse.

98.

99. Project for a Spiral Tower.

100, 101. Projects for a Pyramid.

101.

102–105. Project for a Cenotaph for Turenne.

103.

104.

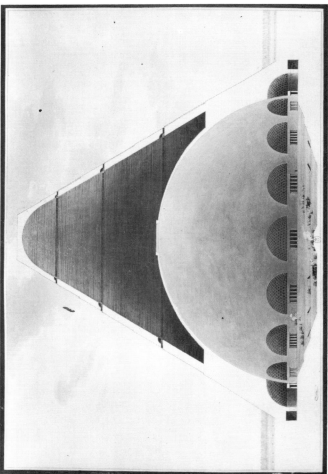

105.

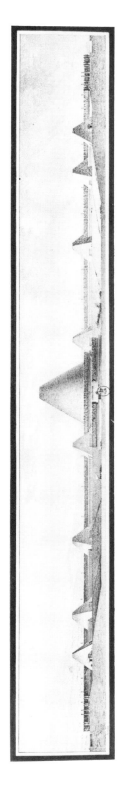

106–109. Project for a truncated, cone-shaped Cenotaph.

108.

110. Project for a Cenotaph "in the Egyptian style."

111. Project for the Entrance to a Cemetery.

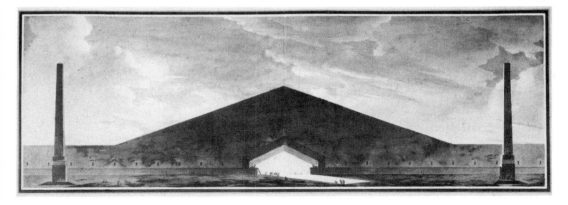

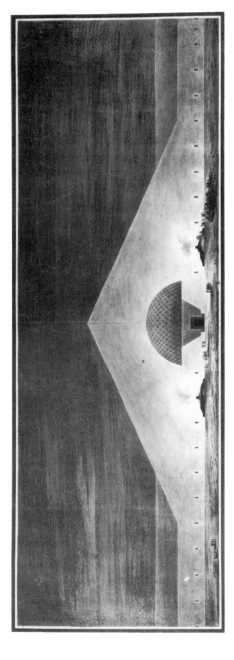

112. Project for a Chapel of the Dead.

113. Project for a Funerary Chapel.

114. Project for a Funerary Monument
"characteristic of sunken architecture."

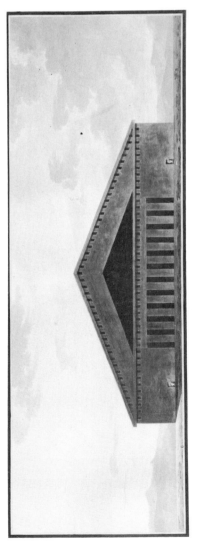

115. Project for a Funerary Monument
"characteristic of an architecture of shadows."

116. Project for a Peripteral Tomb.

117. Project for a Tomb of Hercules.

118. Project for a Tomb for the Spartans.

119. Project for a Monument to the Supreme Being.

de Scipion près Taragone

à St Remi

d'Auguste

Colonne Antonine

à Palmyre

120. Mausoleum of Augustus in Rome,
Jean-Nicolas-Louis Durand, (1800).

Notes

1. *Essai sur l'art,* folios 137 and 144 verso.

2. Abbé Marc-Antoine Laugier, *Essai sur l'architecture,* Paris, 1753.

3. Villar, "Notice nécrologique de Boullée" in *Memoires de l'Institut,* IIIe classe, vol. III, p. 43 ff.

4. On this subject, cf. Jens Erichsen, "Lalive de Jully's Furniture 'à la grecque'" in *The Burlington Magazine,* August 1961; "Marigny and le goût grec", *ibid.,* March 1962; "The Athénienne and the Revival of the Classical Tripod," *ibid.,* March 1963. See also Michel Gallet, *Demeures parisiennes, l'époque Louis XVI,* Paris, 1964.

5. These plans were discovered by H. Colvin and described by R. Middleton in his review of my previous book on Boullée in *Architectural Design,* July 1970, pp. 358–361. They show that some of the conclusions reached in that book must be rectified here, especially as regards the layout of the Alexandre and Monville houses, previously known only from early nineteenth-century plans; it is now clear that by then the original layout had already been considerably modified.

6. The Wrightsman Collection project *(Fig. 29),* brought to my attention by John Harris, is published here for the first time. It indisputedly comes from the Boullée studio, but reveals nothing new about the conception of the Hôtel de Brunoy.

7. *Essai sur l'art,* folio 48.

8. Luc-Vincent Thierry, *Guide des amateurs à Paris,* Paris, 1787, I, p. 90.

9. Thierry, *op. cit.,* II, p. 651 ff.

10. *Biographie universelle et portative . . . des hommes vivants et des hommes morts depuis 1788 . . . ,* Paris, 1834, article on Boullée.

11. This design, in a private collection, was attributed to Ledoux by Raval and Moreux *(Ledoux,* Paris, 1945, *Figs. 256, 257).* It had hitherto escaped my notice. Yet there can be no doubt that it is by

Boullée. Both the style of the drawing and the lettering of titles are characteristic of his designs.

12. *Essai sur l'art*, folio 73.

13. Viel de Saint-Maux, *Septième lettre sur l'architecture*, Paris, 1787, note 29.

14. See our book on Boullée, p. 39; Boullée's set is known from a long and flattering description in the *Journal de Trévoux* (August 1759, pp. 2086–2091). It was engraved with the following inscription: "View of the scenery erected in the College Louis-le-Grand in the year 1759 for the tragedies which precede the solemn distribution of prizes established by His Majesty. Designed by Boullée, arch., Executed by Machy, painter to the King, Drawn and engraved by Poulleau." We have seen only one copy of this print, at a Paris dealer's, our attention having been called to it by Mlle. Monique Mosser. The copy reproduced here lacks the inscription and has a few variants (the copy with inscription, corresponding more closely to the description in the *Journal de Trévoux*, shows a fountain imitating that of Bernini in the Piazza Navona and standing in the central perspective behind the arch of triumph); it is preserved in the Bibliothèque des Arts Décoratifs, Paris (recueil factice, série 79). We are indebted to Mr. Jens Erichsen for the reference to the *Journal de Trevoux* and the identification of the print.

15. *Essai sur l'art*, folio 104 verso.

16. Marie-Joseph Peyre, *Oeuvres d'architecture*, Paris, 1765, introduction.

17. *Essai sur l'art*, folio 142.

18. *Ibid.*, folio 53.

19. Cf. my edition of the *Essai sur l'art*, Paris, 1968.

20. Bequeathed by Boullée to his country, these designs are preserved in the Cabinet des Estampes of the Bibliothèque Nationale, Paris, under the catalogue numbers Ha 55, Ha 56 and Ha 57.

21. These projects are preserved at the Ecole nationale supérieure des Beaux-Arts, Paris. Some were engraved in the *Collection des prix que la ci-devant Académie d'architecture proposait et couronnait tous les ans* (period 1773–1789) and the *Projets d'architecture . . . qui ont merité les grands prix . . . (period 1791–1803)*.

22. *Essai sur l'art*, folio 123 verso.

23. *Ibid.*, folio 70.

24. J.-M. Pérouse de Montclos, "Charles-François Viel, architecte de l'Hôpital général, et Jean-Louis Viel de Saint-Maux," in *Bulletin de la Societé de l'histoire de l'art français*, 1967, pp. 257–269.

25. *Essai sur l'art*, folio 124.

26. This is an unpublished design (pen drawing with India ink wash, 283 x 182 mm.), belonging to M. Jacques Laget, who has kindly allowed me to reproduce it here.

27. *Essai sur l'art*, folio 76 verso.

28. *Ibid.*, folio 70 verso.

29. Manuscript account of Boullée, Bibliothèque Nationale, Manuscrits, fonds français, 9153, folio 38.

30. *Cours d'architecture*, I, p. 186.

31. *Essai sur l'art*, folio 119.

32. *Essai sur l'art*, folios 54, 70, 141.

33. *Essai sur l'art*, folio 127 ff.

34. *Essai sur l'art*, folio 53 verso.

35. *Essai sur l'art*, folio 82 verso.

36. *Essai sur l'art*, folio 126 verso.

37. *Essai sur l'art*, folio 129 verso.

38. *Ibid.*, folio 110.

39. *Ibid.*, folio 111 ff.

40. *Essai sur l'art*, folio 109.

41. Boullée's sympathy with the Revolution did not survive the Terror, and he was even suspected of royalism.

42. *Essai sur l'art*, folio 57 verso.

43. Cf. Charles Dupuis, *L'Origine de tous les cultes ou Religion universelle*, Paris, H. Angasse, Year III [1795], 4 vols.

44. *Essai sur l'art*, folio 90 verso.

45. *Essai sur l'art*, folio 144.

46. *Essai sur l'art*, folio 70.

47. Charles-François Viel, *Décadence de l'architecture à la fin du XVIIIe siècle*, Paris, 1800.

48. Victor Hugo, *Quatre-vingt-treize*, Paris, 1874, Livre III, pp. I, III, "La Convention."

49. Speer, in his memoirs (*Inside the Third Reich*, New York and London, 1970), does, it is true, cite Boullée's example. But did he really have Boullée in mind when he began drawing up his projects in the 1930s? Speer's reference to him looks as if it may be an afterthought, prompted by Boullée's present-day celebrity.

Glossary *

Athénienne   Three-legged piece of decorative furniture, invented in France in the eighteenth century.

Balustrade   A series of short posts or pillars (balusters) supporting a rail or coping.

Barrel Vault   The simplest kind of vault: a continuous vault of semicircular or pointed sections, unbroken in its length by cross vaults.

Blind Attic, Wall   Having no windows.

Capital   The head of a column.

Colonnade   A series of columns placed at regular intervals, and supporting an entablature.

Colossal Order   Any order the columns of which rise from the ground through several stories.

Crepidoma   The stepped base of a Greek temple.

Cupola   A dome, especially a small one, on a circular or polygonal base crowning a roof or turret.

Dome   A vault of even curvature, built on a circular base. The cross section can be segmental, semicircular, pointed, or bulbous.

Elevation   The external faces of a building; also, a drawing made in projection on a vertical plane to show any one face of a building.

Entablature   The upper part of an order; it consists of architrave, frieze, and cornice.

Gable   The triangular or semi-circular upper portion of a wall to carry a pitched roof.

Module   In classical architecture, half the diameter of a column at its base; in modern architecture the term has come to mean any unit of measurement which facilitates prefabrication.

*This glossary was prepared by the editor.

114

Necking Band A narrow moulding around the bottom of a capital, running between it and the shaft of the column.

Oculus A round window.

Order a) In classical architecture, a column with base, shaft, capital, and entablature, decorated and proportioned according to the Doric, Tuscan, Ionic, Corinthian, or Composite mode. b) a series of concentric steps receding towards the opening of a doorway or window.

Pediment In classical architecture, a low-pitched gable above a portico made by running the top member of the entablature along the sides of the gable. Also found above doors, windows, etc.

Peripteral Having a single peristyle or row of columns surrounding it, as a Greek temple.

Peristyle A range of columns surrounding a building or an open court.

Pier A solid masonary support, as distinct from a column; the mass between doors, windows, etc.

Pilaster A shallow pier or rectangular column projecting from a wall and, in classical architecture, conforming with one of the orders.

Portico A roofed space forming the entrance and centerpiece of the façade of a temple, house, or church, often with detached or attached columns and a pediment.

Rotunda A building or room circular in plan and usually domed.

Spandrel Triangular space between the side of an arch, the horizontal drawn from the level of its apex, and the vertical of its springing. Also, the surface between two arches in an arcade.

Springing Line The level at which an arch springs from its supports.

Strapwork An ornamentation which originated in the Netherlands about 1540, and also common in Elizabethan England. It consists of interlaced bands and forms similar to fretwork or cut leather.

Stylobate The substructure on which a colonnade stands; the top step of the crepidoma.

Tholus The dome of a circular building, or the building itself, as in the case of a Mycenaean tomb.

Vitruvian Scroll A classical ornament sometimes used in a frieze; it is similar to a wave ornament.

Volute A spiral scroll on the Ionic capital. Small versions sometimes appear on Composite and Corinthian capitals.

Brief Chronology

of the Life of

Etienne-Louis Boullée

All buildings mentioned are in
Paris, unless otherwise specified

1728   Born in Paris.

1740–1746   Studies under various masters, in particular the
painter Jean-Baptiste Pierre and the architects Jacques-
François Blondel and Jean-Laurent Legeay.

1747   Serves as Professor of Architecture at the Ecole des
Ponts et Chaussées.

1752   Decorates the sanctuary of the Chapel of the Virgin in
the church of Saint-Roch. Designs stage scenery for the
College Louis-le-Grand.

1754   Builds Chapel of Calvary in the church of Saint-Roch, in
collaboration with Falconet and De Machy. *(See Fig. 4)*

1759   Designs initial project for the transept chapels of the
church of Saint-Roch. Designs stage scenery for the
Collège Louis-le-Grand.

1761   Carries out work on the Château du Perreux at
Nogent-sur-Marne (destroyed).

1762   Decorates the house of M. Tourolle in the rue Charlot
(destroyed) *(See Fig. 9)*. At the Academy of Architecture
he presents a project for the reconstruction of the Hôtel
des Monnaies (Royal Mint) on the Quai Conti *(See
Figs. 6–8)*. Admitted to the Academy of Architecture as
a second-class member.

1763   Builds the chapels at each end of the transept of the church of Saint-Roch *(See Fig. 5)* and the house of the banker Alexandre in the rue de la Ville-l'Evêque (now No. 16) *(See Figs. 10–13)*.

1764   Designs project for the remodeling of the Palais Bourbon for the Prince de Condé *(See Fig. 21)*. Builds two town houses for M. de Monville in the rue d'Anjou-Saint-Honoré (both destroyed) *(See Figs. 14–16)*. Rebuilds the Château de Chaville (Hauts-de-Seine) for the Comte de Tessé (destroyed) *(See Figs. 17–20)*.

About 1768   Builds the house of M. de Pernon in the rue de la Chaussée d'Antin (destroyed).

About 1769   Builds the town house of the Baron de Thun in the rue de la Chaussée d'Antin (destroyed). Carries out work on the Hôtel de Villeroy in the rue Saint-Dominique, for the Comte de Tesse.

After 1771   Remodels the house of the financier Beaujon at Issy-les-Moulineaux (destroyed) *(See Fig. 25)*.

1774   Remodels the Hôtel d'Evreux (the present-day Palais de l'Elysée) in the rue du Faubourg-Saint-Honoré *(See Figs. 22–24)*. Builds the town house of Mme. de Brunoy in the rue du Faubourg-Saint-Honoré (destroyed) *(See Figs. 26–31)*.

1775   Is appointed Chief Architect (Intendant des Batiments) of the Comte d'Artois, the king's brother.

1776   Arranges the apartments of the Comte d'Artois in the Palais du Temple (destroyed).

1777   Gives up his post as Chief Architect of the Comte d'Artois. Builds an apartment house in the rue Royale.

1778   Is appointed General Controller of Buildings (Contrôleur général des Bâtiments) at the Hôtel des Invalides.

1780   Converts the former Hôtel de la Force into a prison (Prison de la Grande-Force, destroyed). Project for remodeling and enlarging the Palace of Versailles drawn up for the Comte d'Angiviller, Director of Royal Buildings *(See Figs. 36–37)*. Is appointed to the post of Controller of Buildings at the Ecole Militaire and made a first-class member of the Academy of Architecture.

Project for a Palace for the Comte d'Artois at the Pépinière du Roule (?) *(See Fig. 33).* Project for an arch of Triumph (?) *(See Figs. 83, 84).*

1781   Designs project for an Opera House to replace the hall in the Palais-Royal *(See Figs. 47–51).* Project for a Metropolitan Church *(See Figs. 41–46).*

1782   Gives up his two posts as Controller of Buildings at the Hôtel des Invalides and the Ecole Militaire.

1783   Designs project for a museum *(See Figs. 52–56).*

1784   Builds the entrance to the Bourse in the rue Vivienne (destroyed) *(See Fig. 34).* Designs project for a Newton memorial *(See Figs. 57–59).* Designs project for a public library on the site of the Couvent des Capucines *(See Figs. 62–64).*

1785   Designs project for the palace of a sovereign at Saint-Germain-en-Laye *(See Fig. 72).* Designs project for remodeling the royal library in the rue de Richelieu *(See Figs. 65–69).*

1787   Designs project for a bridge over the Seine (Pont Louis XVI) opposite the Place Louis XV (now Place de la Concorde) *(See Fig. 73).*

1788   Remodels the Hôtel de Langlée in the rue des Petits-Champs for the Loterie Royale (destroyed).

1791   Carries out work on the Hôtel Tubeuf in the rue des Petits-Champs for the Caisse de l'Extraordinaire (Office of Extraordinary Taxes) and on a house in the Place Vendôme for the Direction générale de la Liquidation (Bureau of Debts and Claims).

1792   Designs projects for a National Assembly Hall and a Municipal Palace *(See Figs. 74–80).*

1793   Is appointed a substitute member of the national arts jury. Project for a Temple of Nature (?) *(See Figs. 60, 61).*

1794   Is appointed a member of the jury which judges the subjects set for the competitions organized by the National Convention.

1795   Becomes a member of the Institut de France.

1799   Dies in Paris.

Selected Bibliography

For a detailed bibliography, see J.-M. Pérouse de Montclos, *Etienne-Louis Boullée. De l'architecture classique à l'architecture révolutionnaire*, Paris, 1969. Given below is a selection of books and articles dealing with Boullée.

Sources

Peyre, Marie-Joseph, *Oeuvres d'architecture*, Paris, 1765.

Legeay, Jean-Laurent, *Collection de divers sujets de Vases, Tombeaux, Ruines et Fontaines* . . . , Paris, 1770.

Viel de Saint-Maux, *Lettres sur l'architecture des anciens et des modernes* . . . , Paris, 1787.

Collection des prix que la ci-devant Académie d'Architecture proposait et couronnait tous les ans . . . (1773–1789), Paris, n.d.

Durand, Jean-Nicolas-Louis, *Recueil et paralléle des édifices en tous genres anciens et modernes*, Paris, 1800.

Viel, Charles-François, *Décadence de l'architecture à la fin du XVIIIème siècle*, Paris, 1800.

Ledoux, Claude-Nicolas, L'architecture considérée sous le rapport de l'art des moeurs et de la legislation, Paris, 1804.

Projets d'architecture . . . qui ont mérité les grands prix accordés par l'Académie, l'Institut national de France . . . (1791–1803), Paris, 1806.

Durand, Jean-Nicolas-Louis, *Précis des leçons d'architecture données à l'Ecole polytechnique*, Paris, 1809.

Boullée, Etienne-Louis. *Architecture. Essai sur l'art*, with introduction and notes by J.-M. Pérouse de Montclos, Paris, 1968.

General Works

Renouvier, Jules, *Histoire de l'art pendant la Révolution* . . . , Paris, 1863.

Benoit, François, *L'Art français sous la Révolution et l'Empire* . . . , Paris, 1897.

Bertrand, Louis, *La fin du classicisme et le retour à l'antique dans la seconde moitié du XVIIIème siècle et les premières annèes du XIXème siècle en France*, Paris, 1897.

Klopfer, Paul, *Von Palladio bis Schinkel, eine Charakteristik der Baukunst des Klassizismus*, Esslingen, 1911.

Grabar, Igor, *Alexandrovski Klassitzim i evo frantsouzkie istotchniki*, in *Starie Gody*, 1912.

Hautecoeur, Louis, *Rome et la Renaissance de l'Antiquité à la fin du XVIIIème siècle*, Paris, 1912.

Giedion, Sigfried, *Spätbarocker und romantischer Klassicismus*, Munich, 1922.

Folkierski, Wladyslaw, *Entre le classicisme et le romantisme. Essai sur l'esthètique et les esthèticiens du XVIIIème siècle*, Krakow–Paris, 1925.

Kimball, Fiske, "Les influences anglaises dans la formation du style Louis XVI" in *Gazette des Beaux-Arts*, January and February, 1931.

Kaufmann, Emil, "Etienne-Louis Boullée," in *The Art Bulletin*, Vol. XXI, September, 1939, pp. 213–227.

Kimball, Fiske, "Romantic Classicism in Architecture," in *Gazette des Beaux-Arts*, February, 1944.

Sedlmayr, Hans, *Der Verlust der Mitte, die bildende Kunst des 19. und 20. Jahrhunderts als Symptom und Symbol der Zeit*, Salzburg, 1948.

Kaufmann, Emil, *Three Revolutionary Architects: Boullée, Ledoux, and Lequeu*, The American Philosophical Society, Philadelphia, 1952.

Pariset, François-Georges, "Le néo-classicisme," in *Information d'histoire de l'art*, 1952.

Hautecoeur, Louis, *Histoire de l'architecture classique en France*, vol. 4 (1952), vol. 5 Paris, (1953).

Zeitler, Rudolf, *Klassizismus und Utopia* . . . , Stockholm, 1954.

Kaufmann, Emil, *Architecture in the Age of Reason*, Harvard University Press, Cambridge, Mass., 1955; paperback edition Dover Publications, New York, 1968.

Hitchcock, Henry-Russell, *Architecture: 19th and 20th Centuries*, London 1958.

Reutersvärd, Oscar. "De sjunkna bagarna hos Ledoux, Boullée, Cellerier och Fontaine," with English summary, "The Sunken

Arches of Ledoux, Boullée, Cellerier and Fontaine," in *Konsthistorisk Tidskrift*, Vol. XXIX, Nos. 3–4, 1960, pp. 98–118.

Rosenau, Helen. "Boullée and Ledoux as Town-planners, a Re-assessment," in *Gazette des Beaux-Arts*, March, 1964, pp. 173–190.

Lankheit, Klaus, *Revolution und Restauration*, Baden-Baden, 1965.

Leith, James, *The Idea of Art as Propaganda in France: 1750–1799*, Toronto, 1965.

Harris, John, "Le Geay, Piranesi and International Neo-classicism in Rome 1740–1750," in *Essays . . . Presented to Wittkower*, London, 1967.

Vogt, Adolf-Max. "Die französische Revolutionarchitektur und der Newtonismus," in *Epochen europäischer Kunst*, Vol. I: *Stil und Uberlieferung in der Kunst des Abendlandes* (Akten des 21. Internationalen Kongresses für Kunstgeschichte in Bonn, 1964), Mann, Berlin, 1967, pp. 229–232.

Lankheit, Klaus, *Der Tempel des Vernunft. Unveroffentlichte Zeichnungen von E.-L. Boullée*, Basel-Stuttgart, 1968.

Visionary Architects: Boullée, Ledoux, Lequeu, catalogue of an exhibition held at the University of St. Thomas, Houston, the City Art Museum of St. Louis, the Metropolitan Museum of Art, New York, the Art Institute of Chicago, and the M.H. De Young Memorial Museum, San Francisco, 1967–1968.

Vogt, Adolf-Max. *Boullées Newton-Denkmal. Sakralbau und Kugelidee*, Basel, 1969.

Index

Archives photographiques photo: 5

Bibliothèque des Arts dècoratifs, Recueil factice: 1

Bibliothèque Nationale, Cabinet des Estampes: 8 (Va 262, vol. I); 33 (Va 280); 34 (Va 237, Vol. II); 36, 37 (Ha 56, Pls. 20, 18); 38–40 (Ha 57, Pls. 3, 2, 1); 41–45 (Ha 56, Pls. 2, 4, 6, 8–9); 47–56 (Ha 56, Pls. 4, 7, 14, 12, 11, 26, 28, 29, 31, 30); 57–59 (Ha 57, Pls. 6, 8–9); 62–64 (Ha 55, Pls. 5, 3, 2); 65–71 (Ha 56, Pls. 32, 34, 36, 35, 43, 37, 45); 72 (Ha 56, Pl. 22); 73 (Ha 55, Pl. 35); 74–77 (Ha 56, Pls. 10–13); 78 (Ha 56, Pl. 14); 79, 80 (Ha 56, Pls. 16, 15); 81, 82 (Ha 56, Pls. 23, 25); 83, 84 (Ha 55, Pls. 33, 34); 85, 86 (Ha 57, Pls. 33, 34); 88, 89 (Ha 55, Pls. 18, 21); 90–93 (Ha 57, Pls. 28–29, 32, 31); 96 (Ha 57, Pl. 30); 98 (Ha 57, Pl. 31); 99 (Ha 57, Pl. 32); 102–109 (Ha 57, Pls. 23, 13, 11, 14, 22, 20, 18, 21); 110–112 (Ha 55, Pls. 26-28); 114, 115 (Ha 55, Pls. 29–30); 116–118 (Ha 57, Pls. 25–27); 119 (Ha 55, Pl. 25)

Bibliothèque de l'hôtel des Monnaies, quai Conti: 6

British Museum: 13–16, 26, 27, 30, 31

Catalog of the Pierre Decourcelle sale, Paris, May 29 and 30, 1915, No. 133: 21

Jean-Nicolas-Louis Durand, *Recueil et parallèle des édifices en tous genres* . . . , Paris, Year VIII and IX (1800–1801): 120

Esnauts et Rapilly: 11, 12

Flammarion photo: 9

Giraudon photo: 25

Jean-Charles Krafft and N. Ransonnette, *Plans, coupes et élévations des plus belles maisons et des hôtels construits à Paris et dans les environs entre 1771 et 1802,* Paris, n.d. (1802), Pl. 1: 26, 28

Collection Jacques Laget, Paris: 87

Minutier central des Notaires de Paris (XCII, 662): 17–20

Claude de Montclos photo: 10, 22–24

Musée des Beaux-Arts de Pau, no. 56.3.1: 4

Musée Carnavalet, estampes, topo.115D: 3, 7, 32 ("Projets d'architecte" series)

Piranesi, Prima parte di architetture e prospettive, Rome, 1743: 2

Private Collection: 35

Royal Institute of British Architects, London: 46

Uffizi, Florence, Martelli Collection: 60–61 (6593A–6594A); 94–95 (6588A, 6589A); 97 (6592A); 100–101 (6591A, 6590A); 113 (6587A)

Wrightsman Collection, New York: 29

DATE DUE

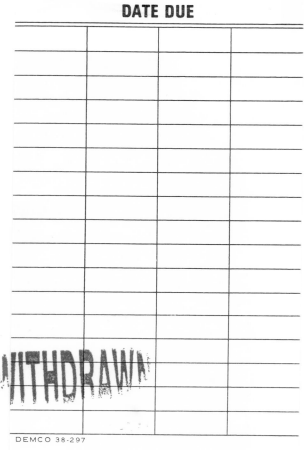
